Living for Jesus
A Biblical Focus for Relating to God's Son

Bible Study Workbook by

James J. Stewart

© 2016 James J. Stewart

ISBN: 978-0-9861334-9-7

Introduction: Following and Imitating Jesus

Being a Christian involves more than accepting some beliefs and trying to practice those beliefs. Unlike other religions, Christianity centers upon having a relationship with God through Jesus our Savior. In our quest to know God more deeply the Bible is our primary resource. The first verse of an old hymn says:

> "Living for Jesus a life that is true
> Striving to please Him in all that I do;
> Yielding allegiance, glad hearted
> and free
> This is the path-way of blessing
> for me."
> – Lyrics by Thomas O. Chisholm

This course is about learning to live for Jesus in an effective and productive way. It does *not* simply focus either upon events in the life of Jesus or upon his teachings. Instead, it looks at some of those events and teachings from a few different perspectives. It is designed for small-group study.

First, we will see how Jesus relates to individuals with His compassion, truth, humility, and authority. Secondly, we will examine how those individuals who heard Him responded to Jesus' impact upon their lives, and how we can do so as well. These situations we examine will uncover the nature and character of Jesus and His will for each of us. Simply stated, this study focuses upon Jesus himself. The Gospel of John focuses upon the person of Jesus that he knew, watching Jesus conversing with people one on one.

The other gospels focus more upon his public teachings, though they also give us some glimpses of Jesus' character. Following Jesus is a lifetime pursuit. These seven sessions are intended to give Christians a fresh or new start in that pursuit.

Session One: Encountering Jesus

ICEBREAKER:
Talk about how the most important personal relationships in your life developed.

▶ **Getting to know Jesus involves learning to like, love, and trust Him.** ◀

Personal relationships are critical to developing knowledge of ourselves and how we fit within the world. It is through interactions with others, we discover how we think, believe, and behave. Some of these relationships are brief, and some last many years. What each of us desires is deep and strong close relationships that help us grow. Studying personal relationships in the life of Jesus allows us to discover how He impacted individual people and see their response to His influence. It also helps us to more deeply consider how we each respond to the presence of Jesus in our life.

Our relationship with God through His Son, Jesus, can reflect the other relationships we have in our culture. The language of our worship music reflects familiar images of our lives as being part of our relationship with God. Our expressions of worship reflect our day to day experiences of work, play, and love. That same worship language also reflects both the boundaries of our everyday living and the freedom we have in Jesus Christ.

 **READ:**
The Word Became Flesh – John 1:14-18

NOTES

- ➢ By becoming flesh in the person of Jesus, John asserts God's redeeming word is fulfilled. God's promises of salvation are personified in Jesus.

- ➢ John gives new meaning to the Greek word, *logos*, translated into English as *word*. It means more than simply speech. It is God's word in action – creating, transmuting, transforming, and redeeming.

- ➢ God has always been Savior, and Jesus is Savior-in-the-Flesh.

- ➢ When John says, "The *word* became flesh and *lived* among us," a literal translation of the Greek says He *"pitched tent with us."*

QUESTIONS FOR REFLECTION

1. When you give your word about something, is it important to you? Do you trust all of God's promises? Why?

2. Have you ever thought about being in the wilderness and having Jesus pitching his tent along side of yours? Does that image help you to love Jesus' presence? Why?

3. Since Jesus has pitched his tent among ours, what does this tell us about getting to know our neighbors?

READ:
The Wedding at Cana – John 2:1-11

NOTES

> ➢ Jesus' address of Mary as 'woman' was one of profound respect in that culture.
>
> ➢ Jesus affirms [verse 4] that the time for His being made known as Messiah was to be determined by God – not by His mother's needs or desires.
>
> ➢ The wedding celebration would continue for days.

> John's term, "signs," denotes those events that manifest God's power present in Jesus

QUESTIONS FOR REFLECTION

1. Was Mary asking a little too much of her Son? Do you like his response to her?

2. As you look at the wedding through Jesus' eyes, does it help you to see Him more clearly as a part of everyday life?

3. Do you think it is important to a Christian marriage that the couple makes Jesus part of their marriage?

 **READ:**
Nicodemus Visits Jesus – John 3:1-21

NOTES

- Nicodemus may have met with Jesus at night so as not to draw attention to himself.
- The Pharisees were totally devoted to The Torah [law] and to the keeping of it.
- Re-birth by baptism was a widely understood concept. When people were baptized into Judaism, they even received a new name as a confirmation of their totally new life.
- Martin Luther called John 3:16 "the Gospel in miniature."
- The reference to Moses can be found in Numbers 21:9.
- The quotation may or may not conclude at verse 16. It may continue through verse 21.

QUESTIONS FOR REFLECTION

1. Do you see Jesus differently in this encounter with Nicodemus than in his role at the wedding? Why?

2. How would you describe Jesus' attitude towards Nicodemus? Do you know anyone like Nicodemus?

3. When you were baptized, did you come up out of the water feeling as though you were a new person in Christ?

NEXT

Be thinking about how you relate to someone who has authority over you. Perhaps you have a boss with whom you try to have a good relationship.

PRAYER:
Heavenly Father, we're glad you
sent Jesus to live among us.
We want to know Him
and draw closer to you.
Fill our lives with
a sense of your presence,
we ask in Jesus' name. Amen.

Session Two

ICEBREAKER:
Talk about how you get to know people you meet who are very different than you are.

▶**Jesus meets us where we are
when we seek Him.**◀

Those being trained as leaders are often told to "meet people where they are." It means figuring out their lifestyles, values, emotions, and needs, and then talking to them on those terms. If a leader does not approach people in this way, they are not nearly as effective. As we study the gospels, we realize that Jesus, who is the ultimate leader, uses this same approach with us. When God sent His son, Jesus, to live among us, it was God's way of bridging the gap between His divine nature and our humanity.

God spoke to Abraham in a dream, giving him images and ideas that were understandable from Abraham's perspective. God spoke to Moses first through a burning bush, and then in the midst of thunder on Mount Sinai. Ultimately, God sent Jesus, to teach us and to live among us. As we read the gospels, we can understand how Jesus continues to meet us where we are when we pray.

 **READ:**
A Conversation in Samaria – John 4:1-26

NOTES

> ➤ Jesus' fatigue illustrates His full humanity, even though He is divine.
>
> ➤ A rabbi seldom spoke with a woman in public, and Jews thought of Samaritans as outcasts.
>
> ➤ A prophet was generally seen as one who could settle religious disputes because they spoke from God's perspective.

QUESTIONS FOR REFLECTION

1. What seems to be Jesus' attitude toward this woman? Would you want to be in her place? Why?

2. How does Jesus meet the woman where she is, beyond his physical presence?

3. How much does Jesus know about you? Are you confident that He accepts you as you are? Why?

 **READ:**
Jesus Walks on Water – Matthew 14:28-33

NOTES

- ➢ This story testifies that Jesus' authority is more than spiritual and political.
- ➢ According to Matthew, evidently they had been waiting for Jesus but decided to start across without Him. They did not see Him until after they had rowed more than half way across.

QUESTIONS FOR REFLECTION

1. If Jesus had stilled the storm before going out on the water, would the disciples have reacted the same way?

2. What were they afraid of when they saw Jesus? Would you react the same way?

3. Peter went out on the water to join Jesus. Why do you think the others did not follow his example?

4. Does Jesus' meeting them where they were in the midst of a storm have meaning for you?

READ:
The Bread from Heaven – John 6:30-33

NOTES

➢ The ***bread*** is vitally important to John's testimony. He uses Christ's teachings about bread as a frequently recurring theme.

> John does not remind us of what Jesus said about the bread and wine in his account of the Last Supper. Instead, he reminds us with Jesus' teachings about His flesh and blood just after this, in verses 53-58.

QUESTIONS FOR REFLECTION

1. An old hymn says that, at the Lord's Supper, we meet Jesus face to face. When you share in the Lord's Supper, do you feel that Jesus is meeting you where you are?

2. Do you like the idea of Jesus meeting us in person in the breaking of bread as a community? Why?

3. Do you seek Jesus' presence when you partake of the Lord's Supper? Why?

NEXT

Be thinking about what you absolutely have to have every single day. Consider the foundational essentials of your life.

PRAYER:
Heavenly Father, we're glad
that you meet us
where we are through Jesus.
Seeing how others interacted
with him helps us
to know him better.
We give you thanks and praise
in his name. Amen.

Session Three

ICEBREAKER:
Talk about the things you need everyday in addition to food, shelter, and clothing.

▶ Our Needs Determine How We Experience Jesus. ◀

People come to Jesus having varying backgrounds and needs. Then and now, some people are simply curious. Some are hurting, and some are purely part of a group for other reasons. People also come to Jesus with a variety of moods. Each person experiences Jesus through the lens of their own experiences. As we read the gospels, we can see that Jesus has a genuine and perfect awareness of every person's point of view. Jesus' attitude is welcoming towards people, unless they demonstrate hostility.

Jesus treats each individual with thoughtful, kind, and genuine interest. As we examine each encounter Jesus had with people, we see Him take differing approaches, depending upon particular needs. Jesus sometimes asked questions so that everyone listening could see the needs at hand more clearly. He kept his language simple and straight forward as He spoke. Jesus kept His responses and actions uncomplicated as well.

READ:
The Healing At the Pool Of Bethesda - John 5:1-15

NOTES

> ➢ References to *the Jews* in John are not anti-Semitic – John was a Jew. Rather, these are

references to the Jewish authorities, who felt threatened by the popularity of Jesus.

➤ Chronologically, this probably takes place during the Festival of Booths, in which Jews remember the years of wandering through the wilderness and living in tents.

➤ Jesus asks the question because the man may have become accustomed to receiving alms and sympathy, and may have long since given up on being healed.

➤ Jesus seems to have dropped back into the crowd to place emphasis on the man who was healed rather than upon Himself.

QUESTIONS FOR REFLECTION

1. Since Jesus is Savior – the Christ of faith – how do you pray when you need saving from sickness or other difficulty?

2. Do you think Jesus had the same compassion for those who were His critics as those who were healed? How does that affect your prayers for acute needs?

3. Was Jesus making things worse for Himself with the authorities? When you pray for someone, does it affect your relationship with them?

4. How did the invalid's attitude affect his expectations of Jesus? When you pray for someone's acute needs, how important is their attitude?

READ:
The Healing Of the Centurion's Servant – Luke 7:1-10

NOTE:
- For Luke's audience, the faith of a Gentile is as important as that of a Jew.

QUESTIONS FOR REFLECTION

1. Why do you think the Centurion sent Jewish leaders to Jesus rather than one of his slaves or a member of his family?

2. Since attitudes towards Jesus are often important, whose were important in this instance?

3. The Centurion saw Jesus as having the authority to heal, even at a distance, so do you personally have that same kind of confidence in Jesus?

READ:
Jesus' Mother and Brothers - Matthew 12:46-50

NOTE

> ➢ So long as a father was alive he had authority over all of his family, including grown children. When a woman of childbearing years was widowed, she was either immediately remarried or was chaperoned by her adult children.

QUESTIONS FOR REFLECTION

1. What attitude do you detect in Jesus as he responds to the question being raised?

2. Was Jesus responding to a real need?

3. Is His love for them any less because of the teaching ministry to which He has been called?

NEXT

Be thinking of the people you have met who live a life very different from yours. Consider how you approach them and communicate with them.

PRAYER:

Lord, we go to you
when we need your help,
but we know that
we need you all the time.
Only you can satisfy
our hunger for what
we really need.
Thank you for hearing our
prayers and answering us,
In Jesus' name, Amen.

Session Four

ICEBREAKER:
Talk about people you know that see life from a very different point of view and how you communicate with them.

▶**Jesus sees the life we lead differently than we do but He understands.**◀

There's an old song by Jim Reeves, where the title sentence says this:

> *This world is not my home,*
> *I'm just a-passing through.*
> *My treasures are laid up*
> *Somewhere beyond the blue.*

In a sense, everyone can say that this world is not our home, including Jesus. While walking on the Earth, He could see both perspectives, but we cannot. Jesus was acutely aware of His environment in Galilee and Judea, and He obviously could relate to the people in a profoundly meaningful way. He saw the people differently than they saw each other because He could also see them through the eyes of His Father in heaven. Christians believe that through divine eyes, Jesus could see life and its struggles from a much broader perspective.

While walking on the Sea of Galilee, others saw the wind and water as alarming and scary. Jesus recognized this, seeing through the eyes of the disciples. At the same time, however, through the eyes of God, Jesus may well have experienced the coolness of the wind on His face, moving through His hair as it flowed through it, feeling it tug at His tunic, even perhaps lifting His spirits higher and higher. To Jesus, the wind may well have felt alive and revitalizing. He could easily have experienced enjoyment in the wind.

Jesus had a profoundly unique perspective, yet, He also lived among us and saw life through our eyes. He experienced normal human emotions, such as being mad, sad, or glad. He also experienced both hungers and hurts. As we get to know Jesus, we begin seeing more of life through His eyes. As we grasp His love and friendship for us, we develop a hunger to be friends for Him.

READ:
Jesus Calms the Storm – Mark 4:35-41

NOTES

- ➢ Jesus is portrayed as having authority over natural phenomena.
- ➢ The varying titles with which Jesus is addressed in this incident show the varying backgrounds of the disciples and their varying attitudes.
- ➢ Sudden storms on this body of water were, and still are, quite common.

QUESTIONS FOR REFLECTION

1. If Jesus was so lacking in fear that he went to sleep, why did the disciples react as they did?

2. How do you suppose Jesus experiences miracles like this happening through Him?

3. In John 14:12-14 Jesus says we will do works greater than His. Have you considered what it means to have this kind of authority through the power of Jesus' name?

 **READ:**
Jesus Heals The Syrophoenecian Woman's Daughter – Matthew 15:21-28

NOTES

- ➤ Tyre and Sidon were northwest of His previous location, and were part of the district of Phoenicia.
- ➤ Being from that area, the woman was a Gentile, yet she addresses Him as the Jewish savior.
- ➤ Jesus emphasizes that His primary mission is to call Jews back to God, but He responds to her expression of faith.
- ➤ There are two Greek terms for ***dogs***. Jesus uses the term commonly associated with the wild dogs that usually inhabited the refuse heaps outside of established communities. When she responds, she uses the other term in referring to herself, which was typically associated with household pets.

QUESTIONS FOR REFLECTION

1. Is your faith either as simple or as powerful as this woman's? How so?

2. How hard would it be for you to humble yourself to the extent that this woman did?

3. Did Jesus see the woman differently when she expressed her faith? Why?

 **READ:**
The Transfiguration – Matthew 17:1-13

NOTES

- ➢ A time of prayer and meditation grows into an entirely different kind of experience.
- ➢ Nearly a week has passed since Peter's confession and affirmation.
- ➢ In being transfigured, the combined testimonies of the gospels indicate that Jesus took on an appearance that transcended His earthly body.

QUESTIONS FOR REFLECTION

1. If you had been there, how would such a radical change in Jesus' appearance have affected you?

2. In light of Peter's desire to build temporary shelters on the mountain, what might you have wanted to do if you had been there on the mountain?

3. How did Jesus see what happened differently than the others?

NEXT

Be thinking about your best friend, and how you relate to that person differently. Consider how that friendship developed, and what influence that friend has with you.

PRAYER:
Lord, We know that you see
the life we lead differently
than we do,
but we are glad
that you understand,
because you came
and lived among us.
Help us to draw closer to you,
and help us to see each other
as you do,
We pray this in Jesus' name.
Amen.

Session Five

ICEBREAKER: Talk about your best friend, and how that friendship is different from your other relationships.

▶Living in Jesus' presence means more than simply observing.◀

Have you ever considered yourself living in Jesus' shadow? Do you want to live in His shadow?

More than anyone else, the twelve apostles lived in Jesus' shadow. He was their best friend and constant companion. There is little doubt that they were in awe of Him at various times while the days passed by. In the midst of teaching people about the Kingdom of God, Jesus encountered many people with many needs. As they carefully listened to what The Master said and quietly observed what He did, the Apostles got to know Jesus and began to behave like Him. Prior to being called as Apostles, each of them was known in terms of their families and their work. Following Jesus, they learned new ways of living and working. While they did not seem to consider it before Jesus returned to heaven, living in Jesus' shadow meant that they gradually acquired his "brand," His way of living and working.

While we want to have Jesus as our best friend and constant companion, He is also Lord of our lives. Then and now, following Jesus means learning to live and work on His terms and doing things His way. What we learn from Him needs to become part of who we are. The values of today's world tell us that we should try to stand out in what we do. Jesus, conversely, often told those who benefited from His presence and power not to tell others what He had done for them. He wanted them to focus on His teachings about God's kingdom. Gradually, Jesus followers learned to keep the focus on God, rather than upon themselves.

 **READ:**
The Healing of a Boy - Mark 9:14-32

NOTES

- ➢ Jesus was interested in actions but did confirm the diagnosis of possession.
- ➢ Jesus seems to stress that healing takes place not because of technique but because of faith.

QUESTIONS FOR REFLECTION

1. What did the Apostles observe and learn?

2. When the boy was healed, whose faith was involved throughout the process?

3. Have you ever seen a miraculous response to prayer? What was your response?

READ:
Casting The First Stone – John 7:53 - 8:11

NOTES

- The one *without sin* in this instance would be the innocent or wounded party in this purported case of adultery.

- The trap was in Jesus having not been presented two witnesses in agreement [Deuteronomy 19:15] with regard to the accusations against the woman. If Jesus pronounced judgment without hearing two or more agreeing witnesses, He would be in violation of the Torah.

- ➤ Jesus' looking down rather than at her during the turmoil was an act of profound respect.
- ➤ Looking up to speak kindly to her could probably have been an act of healing.

QUESTIONS FOR REFLECTION

1. As the Apostles observed this drama, what might they have learned?

2. Have you ever been tempted to go with the flow of the emotions at the moment rather than to act with sound judgment?

3. Why might the Temple leaders take the risk presenting this case without valid witnesses?

4. Was the woman innocent, or simply not found guilty?

 **READ:**
**At The Home Of Martha And Mary
– Luke 10:38-42**

QUESTIONS FOR REFLECTION

1. What do you learn from this about Jesus' ways and point of view?

2. Which person do you feel like the most often – Mary or Martha?

3. Is Jesus's response to both women compassionate? How were the responses different?

4. Does this interaction with the two women help your own walk in faith? How?

NEXT

Be thinking of the places you go where your Christian values are either unimportant or even scorned. Consider how your behavior may be different in those places than your behavior in a church.

PRAYER:
Lord, reading these stories helps us walk with you, and observing how you deal with people helps us realize that we need to do more than study you. Please help us move from knowing you in our heads to knowing you in our hearts; we pray in Jesus' name. Amen.

Session Six

ICEBREAKER: Talk about living within an environment where your Christian values are not honored.

▶Following Jesus means living in the world His way.◀

Throughout today's world, Christians live and thrive in cultures where they are minorities. Christianity began in a Jewish culture and thrived in a pagan Roman one. The Apostle Paul said Christians shouldn't worry about whether non-Christians follow Christian moral teaching [1 Corinthians 5:9-13]. We are to be stern with each other within the church, to follow Jesus in our behavior closely, but not to insist on holding others to the same rules. As with the people of ancient Corinth, Christians have to find ways to live in our pluralistic society without engaging in unnecessary battles with those who are not Christians.

A Barna Research study asked non-Christians whether they viewed the role of Christians in American society in a favorable or unfavorable way. In 1996, 85% viewed Christians favorably. Ten years later, that approval rating dropped to just 15%. Too many wearing the Christian label were not exhibiting the fruits of the spirit described by the Apostle Paul in Galatians. Those fruits include "love, joy, peace, forbearance, kindness, goodness, faithfulness, gentleness and self-control [Galatians

5:22-23]." In this session, we will see how Jesus behaved in a culture more hostile to His teachings than ours is.

READ:
The Little Children And Jesus – Mark 10:13-16

NOTES

- ➢ Jesus' anger arises from the interference with His expressions of love for the children.
- ➢ Jesus affirms the simple trust manifest in children.

QUESTIONS FOR REFLECTION

1. As the Apostles observed Jesus' attitude toward the children and listened to what He said, what did they learn about living in the world His way?

2. Do you seek a child-like quality in yourself when praying? Why?

3. What do you see in a child's natural humility that might be something God wants to see in you and often doesn't?

 **READ:**
Jesus Drives The Money Changers From The Temple – John 2:13-25

NOTE

> ➢ The temple tax was paid with Jewish money, so Roman currency had to be converted to pay the tax.

QUESTIONS FOR REFLECTION

1. Observing Jesus' anger and hearing what He said, what did the Apostles learn about living in the world His way?

2. Do you think this a burst of temper, or was Jesus expressing righteousness fueled by lots of energy?

3. Do you think Jesus momentarily out of control? Have you ever expressed righteous anger?

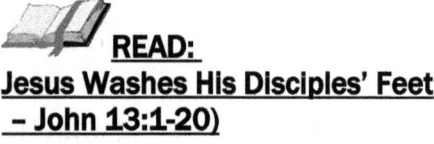 **READ:**
Jesus Washes His Disciples' Feet – John 13:1-20)

NOTES

➢ The rules of hospitality dictated that the host should offer services at the door to make the guests feel comfortable. Those services might include bathing the feet, anointing the head with oil, or offering an embrace.

➢ John makes it clear just how well Jesus knew those who were close to Him.

> Judas is loved and included in the inner circle, even though Jesus knew what Judas was to do.

QUESTIONS FOR REFLECTION

1. What did the Apostles learn about living in this world His way from this act of humility?

2. Have you ever had someone bathe your feet for you? If so, how did you feel?

3. Have you ever felt humbled by someone else's serving your needs in some other way? Did you feel the same way?

4. Do you prefer to serve or to be served? Why?

NEXT

Be thinking about your personal prayer life. Consider what you might need to do in order to strengthen and deepen your spiritual life. Consider also what you may do in order to have a life of prayer that is more satisfying and effective.

PRAYER:
Lord, Jesus, our country is
increasingly less Christian.
Please show us how to bear
the fruits of the spirit
while we live in the midst
of hostility to you,
we pray in your name. Amen.

Session Seven

ICEBREAKER: Talk about whether or not it is important you sense God guiding your prayers.

▶ **Prayer is the living and powerful center of a life that follows Jesus.** ◀

Many people claim that they are "too busy" to spend much time in prayer. The turning point in a Christian's life is often the day they decide to make prayer the center of their life, no matter how busy they are. Following Jesus means pursuing His holiness because ours can never measure up to His. We might make this decision because we sense something is missing in our life. We may also be searching for a way to draw closer to Jesus. It might furthermore be simply that our life seems frustrating or not going anywhere.

Once a Christian decides to put prayer at their life's center, they discover that prayer is more than the completion of a task. It connects Christ with our soul. The result is something intimate and very personal. We cannot fool ourselves with a claim of busyness. Changing that outlook on life requires discipline, which means often sacrificing time for other things that we thought were more important, even including sleep. Try it!

When a Christian puts prayer at the center of their life, they often experience a transformation in every aspect of work, play, love, and worship. They sometimes have more energy and patience. The temptations we've been battling become more easily overcome. They may find themselves wasting less time and complaining less. They may also find it easier to forgive, and easier to avoid fearing the opinions of others. Along the way, it often becomes easier to "find" time to pray. Prayer transforms every Christian life, but to be committed to a prayer-centered life is not easy.

Christian fathers and mothers become the best possible parents to their children when they center their lives and those of their children on prayer. Nothing changes a Christian's life more than the decision to dedicate time to pray. In this final session, we will first look at the longest prayer recorded of Jesus, and then we'll see Him patiently interacting with two men who want His presence. Finally, we will observe Jesus loving and comforting some of his most faithful followers.

 **READ:**
Jesus Prays For His Disciples – John 17:1-26

NOTES
- ➢ This is the most extensive prayer by Jesus in the Biblical record.
- ➢ This is a high priestly prayer in the sense that it intercedes on behalf of all those in His charge.
- ➢ The prayer falls into three sections.

    I Prayer for Himself
   II Prayer for His disciples
  III Prayer for the whole church

QUESTIONS FOR REFLECTION

1. When Jesus prays for Himself [1-5], what is the real focus for His prayer? Is this an example you can follow?

2. When Jesus prays for His disciples [6-19], do you feel part of His focus? Can you pray in this way for the church?

3. Do you learn anything else from this extended prayer?

READ:
Jesus Appears On The Road To Emmaus – Luke 24:13-35

NOTES

- ➢ The conversation seems to center on the difference between differing perspectives of Jesus' identity.
- ➢ Jewish scriptures are traditionally divided into three sections – the law, the prophets, and the writings.
- ➢ Their disappointment in what happened seems to reflect the common expectation of a military Messiah to deliver his people from Roman oppression.
- ➢ There is no indication that they had prayed about what had happened.

QUESTIONS FOR REFLECTION

1. What are some possible explanations as to why they did not recognize Jesus at first?

2. If they had prayed about what had happened, might that have affected their attitude? Why?

3. What are some things we learn in this conversation?

4. Has Jesus' perspective or attitude changed since his resurrection?

READ:
Jesus And A Miraculous Catch Of Fish – John 21:1-14

NOTES
> ➢ Evidently, waiting for the anointing of the Holy Spirit made the disciples restless.

- Peter's leadership is demonstrated in this account.
- Jesus' use of the term **children** may be likened to the term "lads" or "friends."
- In the early-morning hours, sometimes fishermen had spotters on the shore that had a better viewing angle to see the fish.
- John is the first to recognize Jesus in the early light, and he tells Peter and the others.

QUESTIONS FOR REFLECTION

1. If you saw a shadowy figure in the early light, giving you assistance, would you look to see who it was before you acted?

2. After this happened, do you think it became part of their prayer life from then on? Why?

3. If you see God at work in something that happens, does it become part of your prayer life?

NEXT

The Apostle Paul advises his readers to pray without ceasing. It means more than approaching everything in life with an awareness of Christ's presence. With Jesus as our best friend and constant companion, we can approach life with greater courage and faith. Consider working every day to deepen and strengthen your walk with Christ.

PRAYER:

Heavenly Father,
We surrender all of our concerns,
and all that we have, to you.
We are yours, for everything
that you do, you do well.
We lift up to you all the people
whose needs are touching
our hearts.
We give you thanks
for all of our blessings,
especially the gift of
your Son, Jesus,
whom you sent to us.
We lay our sins
at the foot of His cross,
knowing that by His blood, we're
forgiven and redeemed.
We praise you and give you glory
in Jesus' name, Amen.

Other books by James J. Stewart available at Amazon.com and CreateSpace.com:

Christian Poetry, Study and Inspiration
Faith and Yosemite [Christian poetry with pictures]
Faith Fuel
Lasting Love
Walking in Faith
[Editor] **Ephesians: Hope Lives: The Mystery**

Christian Fiction
The Gaardian Saga
Tom's Town
Casting Lots
Prayer Warriors

Yosemite Picture Books
Ever-Changing Yosemite Valley
Faith and Yosemite [see above]
Portraits of El Capitan
Portraits of Half Dome
Starlight Over Yosemite

www.ingramcontent.com/pod-product-compliance
Lightning Source LLC
Chambersburg PA
CBHW060221050426
42446CB00013B/3132